THE
POWER
OF RELENTLESS PRAYER
AND RESILIENT FAITH

DORIS E. GOLDER

THE POWER OF RELENTLESS PRAYER AND
RESILIENT FAITH by Doris E. Golder
Published by D'Vine Strategies LLC
PO Box 20052
Indianapolis, IN 46220

Visit the author's website at www.dvinestrategies. com.

International Standard Book Number:
978-1-7338534-2-2
E-book ISBN: 978-1-7338534-3-9

The author's photo by: Haley Rose Photography

23 24 25 26 27 — 9 8 7 6 5 4 3 2 1
Printed in the United States of America

CONTENTS

INTRODUCTION

ONE OF THE greatest disappointments we experience in our lives is that of unanswered prayers. In many instances, we may feel as if we had suffered a tragedy when our prayers go unanswered. The delays and discouragements can be overwhelming when we feel that the answer did not come when we expected.

We seem to be in waiting mode most of our lives. Are you currently waiting with a friend in the doctor's office to receive the diagnosis from a test result? Or sitting in a courtroom waiting to hear the sound of the gavel return a favorable verdict for your child? Many have been taught at an early age that we have a heavenly Father who loves us—yet when we call upon Him with our needs, He does not always seem to answer. However, this is not the time to lose hope or give up!

Are you aware that the five-letter word *"Faith"* will activate your prayer? When partnered with prayer, faith will move the hand of God to bring the answer to your situation.

One day, I invited a single young mother with two small children to join me at a prayer gathering. She had shared with me earlier that week about her need for additional resources for her family. Yet when she went to inquire, she was turned away. She hesitated, then she said, *"My prayers never seem to get answered. I try to do the right thing. Does God care about me and my family?"*

Do you have similar feelings? *"Does God care?"* Or maybe you have asked, *"Where is God when I need Him?"* Have you become fainthearted because it seems as if God does not care?

For many, prayer is a household word,

universally spoken, yet often reserved for crisis. Jesus instructed His disciples that they were "to pray always and not give up" (Luke 18:1, CSB). The power of relentless prayer and resilient faith will be life-changing to those who persevere in spite of the obstacles we face daily, whether we are waiting to receive an answer to a prayer, or we are being challenged by this journey called life.

The word *power* is defined as the "ability to act or produce an effect."[1]

Are you a veteran to prayer or a new believer who desires to learn more about prayer? Wherever you are in your prayer journey, it is my hope that as you apply the principles within this book, you will be empowered to establish a lifestyle of prayer. I pray that this book will not only change you, but it will also help you influence change in those around you to grasp these truths to change their communities, their nation, and the world.

The biblical story of the widow and the unjust judge is a great illustration to demonstrate the power of persistence through prayer and the resilience to remain strong in a world where disparities and inequality are prevalent.

The word *resilient* is defined in *Merriam Webster Dictionary* as "tending to recover from or adjust easily to misfortune or change."[2]

The beloved parable of the desperate widow is one of the most significant examples of how to receive your answer through faith and relentless prayers.

Just as the widow sought protection from her adversary, we too must fight and resist with the most powerful spiritual tools in our arsenal: relentless prayers and resilient faith. Did you know that there are principles or keys in prayer to help you understand how God operates when you seek Him? When you learn how to apply and activate these keys or principles, they will help to change the course of your prayer life. Watch how your prayer life will soar from mediocre to another dimension.

According to *Merriam-Webster Dictionary*, *relentless* is defined as "not easing up or slackening, maintaining speed or vigor."[3] Relentless prayer is mountain-moving, from the belly-gushing prayers that move heaven and shake hell to remind the enemy to release what God's Word has promised to you. God honors relentless prayers. Apostle Paul encourages us in 1 Thessalonians 5:17 (KJV) to "Pray without ceasing!" This means to push, keep moving, be persistent, and pursue until you receive the answer. Do you have a situation right now that requires relentless prayer? Get ready! Tell the devil that this is his last day to torment you. Reach up and take resilient faith by force, and expect heaven to open and send down the answer to earth.

In the next eight chapters, we will explore the widow's plight for justice from an unjust judge as she pursues help for what appears to be a hopeless situation. We will use imagery throughout the eight chapters to view how this widow refused to be afraid and chose to fight instead. If you desire to have a more effective prayer life, to receive answers, or to learn how to pray the prayers to get answers, this book is written for you.

Learn what strategies the opponent, our enemy, will use to block your answers from being fulfilled and how you can push past those hindrances to get the answers that were there all the time. The Bible reads, "For all the promises of God in him are yea, and in him Amen, unto the glory of God by us" (2 Corinthians 1:20, KJV).

Never settle when God has promised to answer your prayers. Remember, He is a sovereign Master. His character is flaw-less. Sometimes you may experience disappointments while waiting for the answer. My prayer is that this book will help you to see how "No" is not the end of the road or your dream. Always remember that the Master is working things out for your good, and He has success in mind for you. We must stand with resilient faith and trust Him to navigate us through the course that He has designated for our life.

At the end of each chapter, "Reflective Moments of the Soul" is provided for you to reflect on an unjust situation in your past which left a wound that has not healed. How will you respond to this past experience today using prayer and faith as resources? Or how will you apply the principles within the chapters to overcome the scars from this experience so you can become the fulfilled individual that God created you to be? This section may also be used in small study groups. In addition, we close each chapter with a Prayer of Promise to remind you of

God's love and faithfulness as He guides you on the path to receive the answers to your prayers.

If you are ready to receive, I invite you to turn the page and begin your journey to learn more about *The Power of Relentless Prayer and Resilient Faith.*

Chapter One
SETTING THE SCENE

And he spake a parable unto
them to this end, that men ought
always to pray and not faint.
—LUKE 18:1, KJV

A S THE MASTER walked down the dusty roads, from city to city and throughout the countryside, sharing His love and compassion with the people He met, Jesus prayed and searched earnestly for twelve men who would become His students-in-training. His mission was to teach them about the kingdom and God's way of doing things. Under His tutelage, they would become eyewitnesses to the demonstration of His power through signs, wonders, and miracles. In the end, He would endow them with power to do the same. Their lives, as well as the lives of those they impacted, would be changed forever.

Some of the students were reluctant to leave their families and possessions, while others dropped everything quickly and followed Him. The twelve came from various backgrounds and had unique personalities. They were carpenters, fishermen, a tax collector, and more.

The students who followed the Master were part of His inner circle; they were privy to information given only within the group. He called them His disciples, and others were later called apostles, or *"one sent forth"*[1] (Luke 6:13; 9:10). He taught them many things about the kingdom, and one of the most compelling lessons was the power of prayer.

He talked with them about His coming or

arrival, *parousia* (*par-oo-see'-ah*), and the things that would happen before and after His return to the earth.[2]

Jesus wanted them to be on guard, not lose faith, and arm themselves with relentless prayer, so they would not become weary and fall into temptation and away from the purpose that they were to fulfill. Jesus warned them that many dangers and persecutions would occur before He returned to earth but they must not lose hope or give up. He challenged them to stay firm in their faith, and remain persistent in prayer.

No Substitutes

We may use many options and alternatives to provide a solution to a particular problem. However, prayer is not one of them.

Prayer has no substitutes. It stands in a class by itself. First Thessalonians 5:17 (NKJV) encourages us to "Pray without ceasing." The New International Version translates this verse as "Pray continually." You may ask, "How do we do that when we have personal responsibilities, work, and other obligations to fulfill?"

Does this mean that we have to be on our knees praying 24/7? Absolutely not! That would be impossible. The key is to learn to develop a spirit of prayer. This happens when we keep a continuous and vigilant prayer in our spirit that never stops. This can be done daily through meditation or reflecting on the Master's promises in His Word. He is the King of kings and Lord of lords. His ultimate desire is to establish a relationship with you so He can talk with you and you can talk with Him.

Norman Vincent Peale, a minister and best-selling author of *The Power of Positive Thinking,* once said this about prayer, "Pray as you go about the business of the day, on the subway or bus or at your desk. Utilize minute prayers by closing your eyes to shut out the world and concentrating briefly on God's presence. The more you do this every day the nearer you will feel God's presence."[3]

Jesus encouraged His disciples or students not to get discouraged and fall into disbelief when they do not receive an immediate answer to their prayer.[4]

In the mid-1960s, there was a popular long-running TV show called *I Dream of Jeannie* where a genie used powers to make things appear and disappear as she wished.[5]

It is crucial that we do not view God in that manner. God is not a magical genie to be used at our own whim. We cannot put our Master on a shelf when we do not need Him, and then call on Him when a crisis arises. Praying relentlessly is not always easy. It requires discipline. There are times when the Master will answer immediately, and there are other times when we must persevere or persist relentlessly until we receive the answer.

Did you know that we have a covenant right to have our prayers answered? I define a covenant as an agreement between two or more individuals. In this instance, it is a covenant between the Master and you. Within the covenant, there are promises. As believers, His elect and chosen ones who are born again of the water and spirit, we have the right to receive His promises. (See Acts 1:5; 2:38-39.) The promises are His Word and everything He has said about us, who we are, and what He said we could have. Therefore, we can be confident that He will answer our prayers.

The apostle Paul admonished the church to "Be careful for nothing; but in every thing by prayer and supplication [or petition] with thanksgiving let your requests be made known unto God" (Philippians 4:6, KJV). Remember, God's timing is not ours, therefore, delays may come, but He has promised to answer our prayers.

LIFE OR DEATH

My friend, we must pray; it is a matter of life or death. Praying helps us experience the fulfillment of an abundant life that God has promised. Lack of prayer brings about death, where we will not see the manifestation of our prayers, our community healed, or the gospel of salvation proclaimed.

When we have doubt and fear while we are waiting for God to answer our prayers, we are saying, "God is not able to perform what He said." The Master works through our faith. Let us not fall into the enemy's trap of disbelief that God does not hear us and He will not answer. Let us examine how the widow pursued relentlessly with her petition until she received justice (Luke 18:1-8).

THE THIRTY-NINTH PARABLE

Throughout the synoptic Gospels (Matthew, Mark, and Luke), God used parables to illustrate a principle or lesson to the people. The three books share similarities in stories, words, and events of Jesus' life. There are approximately forty parables in the Bible. As Jesus taught, He used parables to illustrate a principle, moral, or lesson to the people. The thirty-ninth parable is about the Widow and the Unjust Judge. This parable teaches us the importance of persevering in prayer. In *Vine's New Testament Dictionary*, the word *parable* is defined as "placing one thing beside another to make or view a comparison."[6] As a result, a "parable illustrates one major truth which consists of several major or minor points."[7]

In this parable, Jesus used this lesson to show His disciples the significance of and need for consistent prayer to accomplish the plans He had for them and to receive answers to their prayers.

THE BELOVED PHYSICIAN

In the Gospel of Luke, the physician described the parable of the widow and the unjust judge. The widow's unrelenting passion and determination to receive justice for her situation were exemplary.

The theme of Luke's gospel focuses on the humanity of God. The church was suffering persecution during this time. Within this book, Luke vividly showed the Master's compassion toward the brokenhearted, the sick, the mistreated, the bereaved, and the lost. He also demonstrated how the Master was concerned about women. Jesus took time to encourage them and minister to them. One woman, who later became part of His following and witnessed His crucifixion, was Mary Magdalene. She was possessed with seven devils, but God delivered her. (See Mark 16:9; Luke 8:2.) Some biblical scholars believe she was a prostitute. However, one of the

Master's attributes is grace. Through grace, He set her free and she became devoted to Jesus and His mission.

As Luke sets the scene to write the eight verses of this thirty-ninth parable, it is interesting to note Jesus' choice of the widow as the key character to illustrate the principles of prayer.

Oftentimes, a widow is seen as vulnerable and defenseless. She is someone who attracts unscrupulous individuals who feed off her helplessness. Luke writes with intensity and passion as he describes the plight of the widow. Only two characters are noted in this parable: the widow and the unjust judge. Yet behind the scenes, there is an invisible Guest who is quietly orchestrating the outcome. Through the widow's dilemma, you will receive the assurance that through perseverance, nothing is impossible when you persist in prayer and stand in resilient faith.

To This End

The three words *to this end* found in the middle of Luke 18:1 (KJV) may leave the reader with the question, "What does this mean, or how do we interpret this phrase?" I believe it means that if the Master has commanded us never to stop praying, then as Mary, His mother, directed the servant at the Wedding Feast held at Cana in John 2:5 (KJV), "Whatsoever he saith unto you, do it."

The word *command* is a military term that is defined according to Dictionary.com as "an order given by one in authority."[8]

The Master has given us a mandate to pray always if we want to see prayers answered, and our purpose fulfilled. Also, we are going to need our resilient faith for the evil days that are coming. Before we close this chapter, it is important that we examine four key words found in this passage of Scripture, which will help us understand this parable.

First is the word *widow*. A widow is a woman whose husband has died. We will elaborate more in chapter 3 on the life of a widow and the challenges she may face without the covering or protection of her husband.

Second is the word *judge*. A judge is a member of the judicial system or court who hears and makes the final determinations for cases that come before them in a court of law.

Third is the word *adversary*. This can be a person, place, thing, etc., that is an enemy or opponent.

Finally, let's look at the word *avenge*. To avenge implies justice. For example, to fight or gain satisfaction for yourself or another's right.

Let us explore further how Luke strategically shows the secret to the widow's success through her relentless prayers.

A Reflective Moment
of the Soul

For a moment, visualize yourself as a student of the Master during His brief three-year teaching term. In that moment, how would you feel as you sit at Jesus' feet and listen to His final instructions prior to His departure? In what way can you take what you have learned from the Master and become an influencer to change the world?

A Prayer of Promise

Jesus, the name above all names, You are the only true and living God. Thank You for being our Advocate and Judge. Your promise says, "Cast all our cares and anxieties on you because you care for us" (1 Peter 5:7, author's paraphrase). Amen.

Chapter Two
WHAT HAPPENED TO RESPECT?

There was in a city a judge, which feared not God, neither regarded man.
—LUKE 18:2, KJV

TODAY WE LIVE in a world where anything goes and people seemingly do whatever they want, with little regard to consequences, the law, or respect to others. This is what many would call disrespect. Injustice appears to be at an all-time high, and if the Master does not make His appearance soon, more decadence will occur.

ATTITUDE OF THE UNJUST JUDGE

In verse 2, Luke introduces the two main characters whose names and the city are not revealed. Within the community, the judge is portrayed as one whose role is significant, yet verse 2 says that this unnamed judge "does not fear God." He did not care, nor was he concerned about the citizens within the city. His character flaws seemed numerous:

- Self-righteous: it was all about him

- Haughty: above reproach, snobbish

- Unjust: He was downright unfair in his court transactions.

He lacked empathy and compassion for the less fortunate. Bottom line, his characteristics point to selfish behavior.

He had no reverence for the Creator, nor did he care about the constituents or citizens that he served within the community (which consisted of the poor and oppressed).

Have you ever had a need so great or a situation that was so life-shattering that you felt that no one understood or cared about what you were going through? Are you experiencing that now? If so, you feel the pain of injustice. Will you let me pray that a shift will come in your situation and that one day, the hurt will lessen and deliverance will come?

> *Heavenly Father, You know the pain that my reader has suffered at the hands of injustice. You are a righteous God and You care deeply about those who are poor, oppressed, the widow, and the orphans. We ask You to lift up the bowed down head and heart of this reader and encourage them to know that they are always on Your mind, and that deliverance will come. You have not*

forgotten them nor will You abandon them. In Jesus' name, amen.

In verse 2, the judge is seen as cold and callous; he appeared ruthless and lacked compassion. As we view the judicial system today, cases come before the court that must be viewed and weighed with accuracy to render a fair verdict. The result must bring a justifiable conclusion to the defendant or plaintiff. The individual who does the crime not only has to be held accountable for their actions, but the returned verdict must also be reasonable for the crime or offense committed.

There are many disparities seen in our world as time draws near for the Second Coming of Christ. Racial inequality appears to be on the rise, as well as attempts to separate (or segregate) races, cultures, and ethnicities. The Creator made it clear in Genesis 1:26 that He sees us as one people who are a reflection of Him. Clearly, there appears to be a constant battle to circumvent God's plans for His creation. However, the clarion call is to "pray always, and not faint" (Luke 18:1, author's paraphrase). The cry is heard from the Master's heart for His people.

Judges During Moses' Times

During the time that Moses was the leader of the children of Israel, judges or rulers were a vital part of the justice system. They had to be honest, fair, and filled with integrity.

In Deuteronomy 16:18 (KJV), Moses instructed the people saying, "Judges and officers shalt thou make thee in all thy gates, which the Lord thy God giveth thee, throughout thy tribes: and they shall judge the people with just judgment."

The judges that were appointed during this time were selected with good moral principles.

Yet this parable informs the reader that the judge found in Luke 18:2 showed no concern for the defendant, who was a widow, or her problem.

Injustice is an ugly word. God hates it! The Bible shows how the Master feels about individuals who are powerful and abuse His people. One such group was the Pharisees mentioned in Matthew 23:14 (KJV):

> *Woe unto you, scribes and Pharisees, hypocrites! For ye devour widows' houses, and for a pretence make long prayer: therefore ye shall receive the greater damnation.*

And Matthew 23:27 (NIV):

> *Woe to you, teachers of the law and Pharisees, you hypocrites! You are like whitewashed tombs, which look beautiful on the outside but on the inside are full of the bones of the dead and everything unclean.*

As we turn to chapter 3, we will witness the unfortunate journey the widow had to experience with the unjust judge, and how she confronted him through continuous relentless prayer and resilient faith to get help for her situation.

A REFLECTIVE MOMENT OF THE SOUL

Have you ever experienced disrespect? Do you still carry the scars today? As the victim, how can you release your accuser so you can live a life of abundance and fulfill your purpose in the earth?

A PRAYER OF PROMISE

Heavenly Father, help me to release any offense that may occur as I push or persevere in relentless prayer to receive my answer. Some may not understand the vision or assignment

I am called to do, and I must not be detoured by distractions. Help me to be sensitive and patient with those around me who need my time as I wait to receive my answer, in Jesus' name, amen.

Chapter Three
THE WIDOW'S PLIGHT

There was a [desperate] widow in that city and she kept coming to him and saying, "Give me justice and legal protection from my adversary."
—LUKE 18:3, AMP

IN 2020, A virus invaded our world with such force that many suffered the loss of family members and friends. It was as if the death angel hovered at each of our doors, and no one would escape its path of sadness. In many states, two-parent homes became one with the loss of a spouse in the wake of this devastation.

By no means do we label this epidemic as an adversary, however, it was an opposing force against our health. *Dictionary.com* defines an *adversary* as "a person, group, or force that opposes…"[1]

The virus was so persistent that it removed approximately "6.5 million individuals from the earth through death."[2]

To date, the pharmaceutical companies continue to seek answers to refine the cure for this virus, just as the widow sought persistently day after day to get help from her oppressor.

HER STORY AND THE OPPRESSOR

Luke continues to write with intense emotion in verse 3, as he describes again the plight of the widow.

In my research of this parable, I was unable to discover the specific problem of the widow. We do know that it was so drastic that she needed legal protection from her adversary, the oppressor. The situation was so overwhelming that she needed the assistance of another person who had a "higher degree of power" to bring her justice. Thus she pursued the help of a judge. She was determined to get a resolution.

Let's imagine what problem the widow may have been facing.

- Was it a large debt that was left by her husband that must be paid immediately upon his death?

- Did she face being evicted from her home and had no place to go? Perhaps she was an only child of deceased parents. Maybe she and her husband had no children.

- Did someone steal her savings, leaving her with very little?

- Was her husband's pension held up for review? I imagine that he was not eligible for pension, and perhaps the guidelines stated that an employee must work ten years to receive a full pension. He worked only nine.

Little did she know that the judge who was assigned to help her was ruthless and uncaring. He did not reverence God nor give consideration or respect even for this widow's plight. She was just another pending case that was on his docket waiting for her name to be called.

It's a dangerous thing to experience the wrath of God, yet the judge had no fear or consciousness of right or wrong.

Oftentimes, we see this in our world today as we witness injustice across the world. Some are calling wrong right, and right wrong, with little regard for our fellow citizens' well-being. God is not unaware of what is going on in the world and to His people. This is His creation. We must hold on through relentless prayers and resilient faith, and we will see God move.

Verse 3 informs the reader that the widow did not go just one time, but went repeatedly asking for his help. Can you imagine being so frustrated after pursuing a situation which required help from someone of a higher authority and receiving nothing?

THE LIFE OF A WIDOW

Oftentimes, widows today are seen as individuals who are vulnerable, and many have been wounded from unscrupulous people who feed off their helplessness. It was discouragement enough that her lifetime partner had died; however, she did not deserve to be harassed.

Yet God has given us specific instructions in His Word on how to care for three specific groups of people: widows, orphans, and the poor. They are under His providential care.

This specific care is divine and blessed to ensure they receive the resources they need.

In Psalm 68:5-6 (KJV), King David reminds us that He is "a father of the fatherless, and a judge of the widows, is God in his holy habitation. God setteth the solitary in families: he bringeth out those which are bound with chains: but the rebellious dwell in a dry land." God's Word has promised that this widow, who was bound in chains of injustice, would be brought out of her dilemma.

In Exodus 22:22-24 (AMP), we read, "You shall not harm or oppress any widow or fatherless child. If you harm or oppress them in any way, and they cry at all to Me [for help], I will most certainly hear their cry; and my wrath shall be kindled and burn…"

Death has no boundaries, nor is it selective. May I pause here and say that a widow can be of any age, with or without children. There are many causes of death. Even young women may experience the loss of their husbands and have to make financial decisions that are crucial to their survival.

A widow, who is older, may have to adjust her living conditions due to her financial status to live modestly. Because of that, she may have several choices.

If she is financially secure, she can choose to stay in her home. If income assistance is needed, she can move into a senior apartment. Or if she has adult children, she can elect to stay with them. Whatever the scenario may be, the widow can oftentimes live a life of uncertainty without the covering or protection of her husband.

Let us look at 1 Timothy 5:3, 5, 9-10 in the Amplified Bible. In this passage, Paul gave insight to the New Testament church on how to honor and provide for the widows in need. I would encourage you to read the entire chapter 5 to gain revelation on how we can reach out to widows who live in our communities and go to our churches to provide resources. Let's look at these selected verses now:

> Honor and help those widows who are truly widowed [alone, and without support]…
>
> Now a woman who is really a widow and has been left [entirely] alone [without adequate income] trusts in God and continues in supplications and prayers night and day…
>
> A widow is to be put on the list [to receive regular assistance] only if she is over sixty years of age, [having been] the wife of one man, and has a reputation for good deeds; [she is eligible] if she has brought up children, if she has shown hospitality to strangers, if she has washed the feet of the saints (God's people), if she has assisted the distressed, and

has devoted herself to doing good in
every way.

Luke does not give exact details of the widow's daily living conditions, but we do know
that she continued to pursue relentlessly to
receive urgent help from the unjust judge.

HAS YOUR FAITH EVER
BEEN SHAKEN?

Can you ever remember a time when you were
interceding in prayer about a need so great
that you felt that if you did not receive an
answer soon, the situation would be hopeless?
As you reflect over your life, there were
times when you took the leap of faith to trust
the Master to answer your prayers. In spite of
the opposition, you stood firm and believed
that help was on the way. You reminded Him
that you are faithful in church attendance,
give tithes and offerings, see to the needs of
others, and pray and read His Word daily;

yet, when the opposing force, the enemy, comes to cast doubt and disbelief while you were waiting to receive the answer, you wondered as tears fell, *"Has the Master forgotten about me?"*

You wonder...

- Will I ever receive my promotion?

- Will help come before the eviction notice goes into effect?

- Can my marriage be restored?

Your faith begins to wane and the spirits of dismay and discouragement set in as your opponent, the devil, hammers that last nail of doubt in your mind. My friend, may I encourage you to reach up and grab hold of that "mustard seed faith" the Master promised you? (See Matthew 17:20.) Don't let go until the answer comes. It's coming. Wait on it.

The widow experienced stress as she waited. She needed immediate help. There was no money to hire a defense attorney to stand with her and plead her case. One theologian believed that she even followed the judge to his chamber from the courtroom and to his home in a desperate appeal for help. Nevertheless, in her anxiety, she failed to remember the key to waiting is to trust in the One that can do something about your problem.

The widow's pursuit of the judge reminds me of the words penned in the Book of Isaiah 62:6-7 (KJV), "I have set watchmen upon thy walls, O Jerusalem, which shall never hold their peace day nor night: ye that make mention of the Lord, keep not silence, And give him no rest, till he establish, and till he make Jerusalem a praise in the earth." Give the Master no rest from your prayers!

This thirty-ninth parable models how we should cry out to God through the power of relentless praying and standing with resilient faith for our needs. He delights to hear from you. Give the Master no rest.

Your story may not be like the widow, however, a desperate situation has occurred that needs an immediate resolution. Can you visualize yourself walking quietly beside the widow to the unjust judge's courtroom to plead your case also?

Have you been given a poor health diagnosis, or are you waiting on an answer from God concerning a move in your ministry? Is your son or daughter a prodigal and you have been waiting for them to return home? Whatever you are facing at this moment, I encourage you to follow the principles or keys throughout the next four chapters. With relentless prayers and resilient faith, the Master has promised to answer with a yes, no, or "it's not time."

Physical and Emotional Stressors While Waiting

Luke does not describe the (physical) trauma the widow suffered as she waited on her situation to change. However, one can only visualize the stress she was experiencing while waiting on the judge to give her justice. Remember that anxiety and worry are not words found in the Master's vocabulary. (See Matthew 6:34.) While waiting for an answer to a prayer, the enemy may speak negative thoughts of defeat which can be manifested through physical and emotional stressors. I assure you, this is not of God.

The scripture does not say she was so distraught that she could not eat. Sometimes, when we find ourselves in a crisis like the widow, we use food as a measure of comfort or we push back totally from food which may lead to poor health.

If we choose to push back or abstain from food for a time, fasting coupled with prayer is powerful. We will discuss this further in chapter 5.

The thought of food may have been the last thing on the widow's mind. Rather than place her trust in the One who created the unjust judge, she began to take her eyes off the problem solver and focused on the "problem," which probably caused her sleepless nights.

I wonder how many sleepless nights did she have while lying in her bed, strategizing a way to alleviate this situation? She may have been awake all night looking for ways to approach the judge so he would not send her away but would help her resolve or bring justice to her life-or-death situation. She probably had no money for legal representation and her last hope was to seek help from the judge who constantly rejected her appeals.

May I conclude, the Master honors fasting. He delights when we fast and commune with Him. He is sovereign and knows what is best for you when you ask. Ultimately, it is important for you to know that fasting prepares us to receive His answer.

The emotional stress of waiting for a resolution that has rocked your world can be overwhelming. However, we must remember, as stated in 1 Peter 5:7 (KJV): "Casting all your care upon him; for he careth for you." This scripture is saying, "I've got this, go to bed and to sleep. No need for both of us to stay up." In the words of Dr. Charles Spurgeon, "Anxiety does not empty tomorrow of its sorrow, but only empties today of its strength."[3]

Luke 18:3 (NIV) shows that she "kept coming to him with the plea, 'Grant me justice against my adversary.'" As a result, she must have felt hopeless and in despair; rejected and isolated.

THE OTHER SIDE OF FEAR IS FIGHT

Imagine with me the following: because of the injustice the widow endured from the judge along with the emotional and physical stress of the situation, she sensed the spirit of fear rising within her.

For a second, she lost her will to continue

to pursue for justice. Maybe she said to her-self, "Nobody seems to care or has even tried to help me." However, she felt a nudge from the Master as He gently reminded her of an incident that occurred approximately a year prior to her husband's death when she needed financial assistance to take care of her hus-band's needs. Deliverance came from an unexpected source. God's ways are not ours.

At that moment, she felt faith rise within her as she remembered the two things she pursued through praying:

- First, she put the Master in remem-brance of His Word. She placed a demand on God with the Word and reminded Him that He promised to provide for her needs.

- Second, she began to speak the answer, not the problem. As you pray, trust God! You may not see a break-through, but the Master is working it out for your good. Have the confidence. Believe God! Proverbs 3:5 (KJV) says, "Trust in the LORD with all thine heart; and lean not unto thine own understanding."

She was determined not to wear the ugly cloak of fear, but to remain resilient in faith and fight for deliverance! May I share the story of a friend whose life was held in the balance as he wrestled with three bouts of cancer? The enemy, his adversary said, "Three strikes and you are out!" The Master reaffirmed His promise, "Not so, watch me work a miracle."

His Story: Three Strikes and You're Out

The attacks with cancers began at the age of 60. As a three-cancer survivor, I stood strong in faith for my deliverance. Each time a cancer ravaged my body, I became weaker.

The cancers of Non-Hodgkin's Lymphoma, Colon, then Prostate Cancer invaded my cells and ravaged my body. Other problems began to manifest such as Diabetes and Chronic Kidney disease, however, I was determined to live and fought back through prayer. My strength began to wane but I refuse to give up. Other intercessors joined in praying for me that my faith would not fail. As the cancer progressed, my hair fell out, eyebrows fell off, eyes dulled, skin darkened, but I refused to allow the enemy, the opposing force, speak defeat to me. My team of prayer warriors never stopped praying. I cried out with the last strength within my weakened body, "God, you promised to be my healer!" One year later, I became cancer free. Can the Master heal? If he did it for me, he can do it for you.

(Testimony given by BW)

The same way my friend stood and pursued, the widow also refused to run, but she persevered. If you are faced with an unyielding or invincible situation that makes you feel defeated, do not give up! Be relentless in prayer and stand resilient in your faith. Help will come. In chapter 4, we will explore some of the keys or principles the widow used in receiving her answer that you can apply to receive victory.

A Reflective Moment
of the Soul

Have you ever been ignored or made to feel insignificant? In that moment, you may have reacted in three ways: you experienced hurt, became angry, or you were in denial. Injustice stinks. As you reflect on the incident, how would you react differently now? Have you moved forward or has the residue became part of the present?

A Prayer of Promise

Heavenly Father, You created me after Your image and likeness. You know the number of hairs on my head. You know everything about me. Do not let me be consumed by daily menial activities that will cause emotional and physical stressors to deplete me from fulfilling the call that You have on my life. Your Word says, "Take no thought about tomorrow because it would take care of itself" (Matthew 6:34, KJV, author's paraphrase). Help me to remember that You are my present help when situations get out of control in my life and to trust You until I receive the answer to my prayer. In Jesus' name, amen.

Chapter Four
BEING RELENTLESS PAYS OFF

And he would not for a while: but after-
ward he said within himself, Though
I fear not God, nor regard man.
—LUKE 18:4, KJV

THE POPULAR WORDS, "First Impressions are lasting," have been spoken to me on several occasions. In fact, this was one of my mother's favorite phrases to my siblings and me as we left home to attend university or begin our life careers, "You only get one chance to make a first impression, so be on your best behavior and always look or dress appropriately for the occasion," she would add.

Phil McAleen once said, "From the first word you hear a person speak, you start to form this impression of the person's personality."[1]

The widow had already formed an impression about the judge the first time they met. She was appalled at his behavior as a judge, as he was someone who was given the responsibility to help the citizens in the city to receive justice. Her first impression was negative. He was arrogant, rude, and callous.

He was resistant to her appeal for assistance as she continued to pursue. As believers, we cannot become so insensitive to one another that we miss hearing the cries of those in need. We may not be able to help them with a solution, but we can provide comfort and prayer. The lack of concern for each other does not exemplify the character of the Master.

The Keys to Her Victory

The intention of the unjust judge was never to give the widow what she wanted, but to continue disregarding her cry. However, with her relentless prayers, eventually he granted her a release from her adversary.

Her persistence paid off. Scripture does not say she actually threatened him, but her continual persistence wore him out. Every time the judge looked up, the widow was there. Can you imagine how agitated he had become from her constant requests?

Remember, the judge's credibility was at stake, although it appeared that he was not concerned about what others thought about him. By now, the community where the widow lived had heard her story and was possibly angry at the judge because of how he had treated this widow and offered her no help. Despite all the murmurs and whispers from the citizens, the judge was unmoved.

Ultimately, she wore him out with her continual pursuit and persistence, and suddenly he rendered her justice.

May I ask are you persistent in your petition before the Master? This does not mean that you have to literally cry about your situation or circumstances day and night, but do stand firm in faith and confidence that your heavenly Father heard you and will answer according to His will. It's not how many times you go to Him—He heard you the first time—but you must trust and believe that He will deliver.

Although this is a parable, the widow illustrates a few of the principles we need to act on today. She persisted in going to the unjust judge, waiting to receive help from the situation that oppressed her. The Master has also given us principles in His Word, and if followed, He promised that you will receive the answer that He desires for you.

ASK, SEEK, AND KNOCK

He left one set of keys to relentless prayer in Matthew 7:7 (KJV, emphasis added), "*Ask*, and it shall be given you; *seek*, and ye shall find; *knock*, and it shall be opened unto you..." Jesus gave us three dimensions on how we should pray progressively. Using the acronym ASK, we will explore them.

1. **A**sk. To ask is to make your request known to the Master in prayer. Oftentimes, a prayer to ask Him for provision, such as food, clothes, and shelter is simple. Why? Because He knows we have need of these things.

   However, what if you have approached Him with a specific petition and you are still waiting for an answer? Pause, and then ask yourself, "Am I asking according to the Master's will for my life?" If so, while you wait, find a promise in His Word that aligns or comes into agreement with your petition and confess it every day. If the answer still has not manifested, proceed to the next dimension, which is seeking.

2. **S**eek. To seek is a phrase that conveys something is lost and must be found. In this instance, there are times that the Master does not answer your request quickly. The request may be held up or things are being repositioned for your good. For instance, your desire to have a new beginning has not been answered. God is omniscient. In other words, He knows everything. In the Book of Isaiah 46:9 (NIV), the writer reminds us, "Remember the former things, those of long ago; I am God, and there is no other; I am God, and there is none like me."

Be encouraged; He makes known

the end from the beginning and knows if this is the time for you to move forward—and He knows what lies ahead of you. You are His child and what concerns you, concerns Him. He knows the city where you desire to relocate and for what purpose you are going. Is it possible that He has you "seeking" to draw closer to Him through intercession? Our heavenly Father is not going to do all the work; He needs you to partner with Him in this special request to sense and appreciate the value of the answer. Could it be that He desires you to take your "mustard seed" faith, which is the only amount the Master says we need, and stand firm until the answer manifests itself? As you continue to wait for the answer, let's step up the intensity and move to the final prayer dimension.

3. **K**nock. According to Dictionary. com, the word *knock* is "to make a pounding sound."[2]

Have you ever knocked on someone's door more than once? This may be evidence that they are not at home. Do you knock again or leave? If you leave before they answer, you may experience more of a delay to receive the information needed. To knock is the very essence of the Master's heart. He desires and delights to commune with you. In the example demonstrated in seeking, the individual who desired to relocate to another state for a new beginning must knock again. I wonder what would happen if they were to go back to the prayer dimension of "seek" or to inquire of God about His desire concerning this petition, then wait patiently as He speaks?

As always, God answers with a yes,
no, or "it's not time."

Be persistent with your petition. With some prayers, you may have to wrestle relentlessly as Jacob did in Genesis 32:24-26 (KJV), until Jacob said, "I will not let thee go, except thou bless me."

Just like the widow received the answer to her prayer for justice through persistence with the unjust judge, you can experience victory in receiving answers to your prayer as well. I would like to share with you an aha moment the Master downloaded to me while in meditation. He gave me several more keys that shifted my prayer life to yet another dimension in Him. Should you choose to adapt them as part of your prayer journey, they will change your life too. Let's turn the page and enter the Prayer LAB.

A Reflective Moment of the Soul

Is there a time where you made a bad impression and regretted it? It's never too late to try again. Do not let the ugly spirit of fear delay you from seizing the moment to walk in your destiny. If given another opportunity, what would you do differently?

A Prayer of Promise

Jesus, let me not live with regrets from yesterday. I desire to live each day in abundance and to know that when I pray, You hear me. My delight is to know You and to embrace the covenant promises that You have for me. I will never give up! From this day forward, I will push forward and persist in relentless prayer. Thank You, Master. Amen.

Chapter Five
THE PRAYER LAB

And this is the confidence that we have in him, that, if we ask any thing according to his will, he heareth us: And if we know that he hear us, whatsoever we ask, we know that we have the petitions that we desired of him.
—1 JOHN 5:14-15, KJV

ONE DAY WHILE sitting quietly in His presence, I asked God again, "Why do some of my prayers go unanswered?" I understood the dimensions of prayer by using the acronym ASK: ask, seek and knock. Furthermore, I accepted that my prayer will be answered with a yes, no, or "it's not time."

At that moment, I sensed an urgency that

the Master desired to talk to me. Suddenly, I looked up to see the heavens opened. In the spirit, I saw a white canvas come down before me with the word *LAB* written in red. Quickly, I asked the Master, "What does this mean?" Then I remembered my high school chemistry class and the sleepless nights I stayed up to memorize the parts of the periodic element table that I was required to know before I could move to my junior year.

THE AHA MOMENT

Most high schools require students to take several science courses. One of these courses is typically chemistry.

The objective of the chemistry course is to give the student a basic understanding of chemicals and how they interact with other substances. It is amazing how "chemistry plays a role in every part of our life."[1] Within the curriculum (guidelines), the students are assigned several activities which will consist of experiments in a laboratory to ensure that the student understands and can apply the principles of chemistry.

We are not comparing this chemistry scenario to the principles of prayer, but rather to the process of how infusing certain elements together in a spiritual laboratory will create a powerful prayer life. These elements are represented by the acronym LAB. It is my hope that you will be blessed as you use the Prayer LAB and become victorious as you receive your answers.

The first letter of the acronym L stands for learn. The second letter is A and it stands for abide. The final letter of the acronym is B, and it stands for believe. We will discuss each one in detail to help you gain an understanding of how to use these elements in your prayer life.

- **LEARN** Him. We must know God. As we learn the Master, we will begin to understand more about Him. We will understand His way of doing things, His heart and how He feels about us, and the plans that He has for our lives. Read His Word to learn about His promises and the relationship He had with the biblical saints, prophets, and the ordinary people He met. To know Him is to enter into a relationship. Two people in a relationship cannot know each other until they talk, observe each other's mannerisms, and learn likes and dislikes. As you get to know Him, it will become easier to stand resilient in faith despite the storms that come to weaken your strength. Always remember, He is your heavenly Father, and what concerns you, concerns Him.

God desires to give you good gifts and for you to experience success in your spiritual and physical life. Matthew 7:11 (KJV) reads, "If ye then, being evil, know how to give good gifts unto your children, how much more shall your Father which is in heaven give good things to them that ask him?"

Since we know that God gives us good gifts and wants us to experience success, let's look at some of His attributes as they relate to prayer.

» **He is supreme**. He is the CEO of the universe. He is in control of everything. Nothing surprises Him nor is He caught off guard. Therefore, He knows how to guide your situation and answer your prayer. He is omnipotent. He has unlimited power that you can tap into at any time. He has made it available to you, His child.

» **He is unchanging**. The Master never changes. Malachi 3:6 (KJV) reads, "For I *am* the LORD, I change not." Remember, He "is the same yesterday, today, and forever" (Hebrews 13:8, NLT). You can depend on Him; He is faithful. If you were to interview the following biblical characters, they would tell you that God answered their prayers:

  › The woman with the issue of blood who bled for twelve years until she touched the Master and was made whole instantly (Luke 8:44).

  › The centurion, whose servant was sick; He went looking for the Master to heal his servant. The centurion felt unworthy for Jesus to come to his house, so he asked Jesus to just speak

the Word and his servant
would be healed (Matthew 8:8).

› The blind man who asked
Jesus to restore his sight. The
Master responded and said,
"Go thy way; thy faith hath
made thee whole" (Mark 10:52,
KJV). The Bible says the man
received his sight immediately.

If God can answer these prayers,
then your answer is on the way! Here
are a few more attributes of God.

» **He is faithful**. "Know therefore
that the Lord thy God, he *is* God,
the faithful God, which keepeth
covenant and mercy with them
that love him and keep his commandments to a thousand gen-
erations" (Deut. 7:9, KJV). He is
merciful to you and keeps His
covenant. God will answer the

prayer you have brought before Him when it aligns with His will for your life.

» **He is love.** Sarah Christmyer, in her book *Create in Me a Clean Heart: Ten Minutes a Day in the Penitential Psalms*, writes:

"Because of God's immense love for us we can throw ourselves on him in our pain, whatever its source, even in the self-inflicted pain of sin. We can cry, we can yell, we can beg like a child when it screams 'Mom!' at the first sign of trouble, who assumes she can and will help. God can and will help, and he wants to."[2]

It is unimaginable how much the Master loves us. Apostle Paul wrote, "Who shall separate us from the love of Christ? *shall* tribulation, or distress, or persecution, or famine, or nakedness, or peril, or sword?" (Romans 8:35, KJV)

» **He is holy.** We live in a fallen world, with many people who are indecisive; some have situations that are problematic, and some appear to have no respect for life. In the midst of this chaos, we have a Holy God who is pure, divine, and alive, and Who cares about mankind and their need to have answered prayers. I Samuel 2:2 (KJV) speaks about His character, "There is none holy as the LORD: for there is none beside thee: neither is there any rock like our God."

As you begin to know or learn the Master's character, you will see that anything is possible. In the words of John 15:7, "If ye abide in

me, and my words abide in you, ye
shall ask what ye will, and it shall
be done unto you" (KJV).

* **ABIDE in Him.** The second element in the Prayer LAB is Abide.
According to Merriam-Webster's
Dictionary, the word *abide* is defined
as "to remain stable or withstand."[3]
Apostle John is the author of the
Gospel that bears his name, John. In
John 15:4-7, the apostle used imagery
to illustrate the significance of a plant
called a vine. The vine, or true vine,
is portrayed as our heavenly Father
and the branches that connect to the
vine are the believers.

As Jesus talked with His disciples,
He reminded them to stay attached to
the vine, stay close, remain faithful to
Him so the fruits of the Spirit would
be seen in their lives and they would

bear much fruit. Futhermore, He said to them, "If you become separate from Me, then I will not abide in you and you cannot do anything in and of yourself and will become useless. If you stay with Me and be attentive to my words, watch Me work miracles in your lives according to My will and My timing" (author's paraphrase).

He reminded them of the words He spoke earlier in John 14:12 (KJV) that reads, "Verily, verily, I say unto you, He that believeth on me, the works that I do shall he do also; and greater works than these shall he do; because I go unto my Father."

My friend, with this promise, move forward and cast down the spirit of doubt and defeat right now. Let's reach up and grab hold of faith to see our prayers answered.

May I share four keys to gain momentum to receiving an answered prayer?

» **Have faith.** Faith is the heartbeat of God. In Hebrews 11:6 (KJV) we read, "But without faith it is impossible to please him: for he that cometh to God must believe that he is, and that he is a rewarder of them that diligently seek him."

How do we obtain faith? Apostle Paul says in Romans 10:17 (KJV), "So then faith cometh by hearing and hearing by the word of God." We receive faith by hearing the preached word, reading about the biblical saints who receive miracles in their lives, and listening to individuals of like faith today who share their testimonies of what God has done for them. As a result, this will motivate us to stand in faith and watch the Master work on our behalf.

As the widow continued to seek justice, she looked for the answer from the unjust judge, who relied on the judicial system for the verdict, rather than the almighty God who has the final say.

» **Know His will**. In Matthew 7:11 (NKJV) we read, "If you then, being evil, know how to give good gifts to your children, how much more will your Father who is in heaven give good things to those who ask Him."

As a parent, I delight in giving my adult son nice gifts to celebrate his accomplishments. Likewise, our heavenly Father receives more joy in giving you blessings when you come and ask according to His will.

He is a righteous God and He desires that His children be in right standing with Him as we ask Him for help. Study and embrace His Holy Word, which is His Will, find the promises for your situation, then speak His Word back to Him. Be assured, He desires that your body be healed, mind be healthy, business be successful, family be happy, and much more.

» **Be specific.** The first time you present your petition or request to God, be precise. Luke 18:3 (KJV), says the widow presented her case before the unjust judge with a heartfelt cry, "Avenge me of my adversary." She was specific and direct in her request. She did not doubt but stood firm. James

1:6 (NIV) admonishes us, "But when you ask, you must believe and not doubt, because the one who doubts is like a wave of the sea, blown and tossed by the wind." The widow stood in resilient faith. At some point during her pursuit of the judge, she refused to allow circumstances around her to dictate her outcome. With determination, she forged ahead and continued to be persistent.

» **Activate your faith**. The word *activate* here is used to encourage you to move and be aggressive in your faith. You may be asking, "How do I move in my faith to get my prayers answered?" One way is through confession. Jeremiah 33:3 (KJV) urges you to, "Call unto me and I will answer thee, and shew thee great and mighty things, which thou knowest not." When you speak the promises of God back to him, you activate the ministering angels, who are God's messengers, to move quickly on your behalf and according to God's will return the answer you desired of Him.

- **<u>BELIEVE</u> Him.** This is the third and final element in the Prayer LAB. We must have confidence in God's Word. In Mark 11:23 (NKJV), we read, "For assuredly, I say to you, whoever says to this mountain, 'Be removed and be cast into the sea,' and does not doubt in his heart, but believe that those things he says will be done, he will have whatever he says."

Confidence is the assurance, without doubt or disbelief, that God will do what He said. Doubt and disbelief are the two strategies of Satan to block God's plans to answer your prayer. Faith is a cousin to belief. To have faith, you must believe. You cannot have one without the other.

Dictionary.com defines *faith* as "confidence or trust in a person or thing."[4]

Hebrews 11:1 (KJV) reads, "Now faith is the substance of things hoped for, the evidence of things not seen." According to Dictionary.com, the word *believe* is defined as "having the confidence in the proof."[5]

Before we can move on, let's define *proof.* Dictionary.com says *proof* is "evidence sufficient to establish a thing as true, or to produce belief in its truth."[6]

In 1 Samuel, we find the story of Hannah and how she desired to have a child (1 Samuel

1:5-21). The passage shows how relentless prayer and resilient faith works together. Hannah had a sorrowful spirit. Her adversary or opponent Peninnah, who was the second wife of her husband, Elkanah, continually provoked her because she had no children. This caused Hannah much distress. One day, she went to the House of Shiloh and laid out before God with sincere intercession about her request.

She prayed with such travail that Eli, the priest, thought that she was drunk.

When your spirit is crying out for an answer to a prayer that has been in your belly for a long time and it needs to come forth in birthing, you may appear drunk to others, but you are warring in the heavens to bring the answer to earth.

Hannah was a woman of faith, and she believed that God could open her womb. He answered! She conceived and gave birth to the prophet Samuel. What opponent are you facing that prevents you from receiving your answer? Wrap your prayer with resilient faith and believe. Watch the Master work. If God's Word said it, He cannot lie.

There are many promises in the Bible that affirm God's Word about the desired answer to your prayer. One of my favorites is found in Mark 11:24 (kjv), which reassures us with these words: "Therefore I say to you, What things soever ye desire, when ye pray, believe that ye receive them, and ye shall have them."

Do you have confidence that He has heard you? If so, lift your hands and heart in a spirit of thanksgiving and expect the answer at any moment.

Thanksgiving!

No matter what the situation looks like, there will be times when it seems that God is not working or that He has forgotten you. Yet He is behind the scenes repositioning and preparing you to receive the answer.

Did you know that thanksgiving is a form of worship? The Master dwells in the praises of His people. Psalm 116:17 (KJV) says, "I will offer to thee the sacrifice of thanksgiving, and will call upon the name of the LORD."

While you are waiting and giving thanks to the Master, prepare yourself. If you desire to attend school, explore what schools are available for your interest. Set an appointment to shadow someone in that field to learn how it operates. This can be done in other areas of interest, too. You are simply preparing yourself to receive your answer.

EXPECTANCY THROUGH WORSHIP

There must be an expectancy that you will receive an answer. When God delays your answer, it is for your good. Continue to pray, and meditate on His Word to prepare for the answer when it comes. It may not be in your time, but God has a timetable that is always best. The three elements within the

Prayer LAB are vital to your prayer growth. Continue to trust Him to take you to new places in Him that you desire to go.

HIS PROMISES ARE GUARANTEED

Are there any promises that you are standing on as you move into relentless prayer? The answer is yes. The widow gathered momentum as she visited the judge continually. She may have visited his courtroom just one time a day; however, when she saw his indifference to the urgency of her situation, she renewed her determination to shatter his complacency. The Scriptures say in Luke 18:5 (KJV), "Yet because this widow troubleth me, I will avenge her, lest by her continual coming she weary me."

In other words, the widow bothered him. She annoyed and irritated him.

This unjust judge became distraught by the widow. She didn't just trouble him, but her consistency in troubling him took a toll as well.

Just imagine, she was so desperate that she may have visited him three times a day for five times a week, which totaled fifteen visits. What if she found out where he lived and the parking garage where he parked his car, so she could plead for him to avenge her of her adversary continually?

In today's world, if an individual goes to this length, there would be other ramifications to suffer. However, the widow was so desperate that her situation called for desperate measures.

My friend, I wonder what would happen if we persist in prayer as the widow pursued the judge. Not that we would persist with a repetition of words or asking the same request over and over, but we would persist with a heart of thanksgiving for the answer as we wait with a spirit of expectancy. Our prayers would be answered by the almighty

God because He is our King and He delights in doing good things for His children. This is a promise that is guaranteed. Praise God!

I challenge you to continue to pursue in prayer for a situation, a condition, or a mountain that you have been facing. God promises to answer you. In the next chapter, we will discuss the importance of movement toward God's answer to prayer. You can decide to sit on the sidelines and cheer or get up and be part of the game.

During my tenure as a school counselor, I heard the cries from families who stood in line at a food bank to receive assistance, just to be turned away when the voice on the loud speaker announced that all the food on the shelves was gone.

The adversary or opposing force to them was the lack of food. The families that were turned away did not have an alternative and did not see an end in sight. Just like the widow, the unjust judge was the opponent.

The widow kept going to him, asking and oftentimes demanding, that he grant her justice. Yet he kept refusing. This judge had no mercy nor compassion towards the widow.

We must learn to be relentless in our prayers and advocate for others who are in need. Just as the widow kept pursuing the judge to give her protection and release her from this situation, we as His children must continue to persist relentlessly until we receive the answer to our situation.

My friend, meet me in the Prayer LAB and watch the Master work on our behalf even more. Bring those hard places that need a breakthrough. Be sure to remind Him Who He is. He loves to have you call Him faithful, supreme, and unchanging. When we move, things begin to happen, as we will observe in chapter 6.

A Reflective Moment of the Soul

What is that "hard thing" that you are believing God for a breakthrough? Which letter of LAB (**L**earn, **A**bide, and **B**elieve) is challenging for you in prayer? Take one of these letters and begin to use the principles through prayer in your life for one week about a situation where you need to see a miracle. My friend, watch the Master work. Don't forget to send us a praise report!

A Prayer of Promise

Heavenly Father, I will confess that at the name of Jesus, no demon from hell shall rise up against me. I will confess Psalm 91:10 (KJV), "There shall no evil befall me, neither shall any plague come nigh my dwelling" (author's paraphrase). I will stand resilient in faith to resist the enemy who comes only to abort my assignment, mission, or purpose that You have created me to fulfill. I speak protection over our family, our neighbors, friends, and community, in Jesus' name, amen.

Chapter Six

NOTHING HAPPENS UNTIL YOU MOVE

*Yet because this widow troubleth
me, I will avenge her, lest by her continual coming she weary me.*
—LUKE 18:5, KJV

ALBERT EINSTEIN WAS one of the greatest physicists of the twentieth century. His main focus was theory and not actual facts of research. Einstein is often credited with having said, "Nothing happens until something moves."[1]

As I've already stated in this book, the field of science has never been one of my strengths.

However, I am an avid reader of the theorists and admired those who have contributed so much to our world.

I am sharing Einstein's statement to reference the effectiveness of movement when praying relentlessly.

Did you know that movement can change one's thought process, career, or even destiny? Have you experienced success where you are right now? Do you feel fulfilled? If not, it may be time to move. This is what the widow did. She knew that if she stayed in the same place, her situation would not change.

Her plea was heard! It is noted in verse 5 that the judge consented to help the widow because he got weary of her "continual" visits, and not that it was the right thing to do. In this instance, the judge only thought about himself.

We will apply the statement, "Nothing happens until you move" to the power of relentless prayers and resilient faith. Remember, the widow increased her visits to the judge's courtroom when she saw his resistance to help her.

We can choose to sit and do nothing, or get up and move when we see that we have not received the answers to our prayers. As a reminder, God's time is not our time. My friend, please do not jump ahead of God to help Him. Go back to the Prayer LAB and read about His attributes, and then wait on Him.

If there is a current situation in your life that appears to be stuck, here are three action steps to consider as you move while waiting in the Prayer LAB:

- **Enact a partnership agreement**. The action of agreement is powerful. Find another individual of like faith and whom you trust who will stand strong with you for your situation (without wavering). They must be in agreement with you through prayer and the promises found in God's Word concerning your situation.

• **Fast**. I have mentioned the discipline of fasting several times in this book. At times, fasting appears to be a lost discipline within Christendom. However, it works! When you have a need or a crisis that calls for desperate action, try fasting. It will break strongholds and bring deliverance. When you give up a meal, use the mealtime to turn off television, back away from social media, turn your cell phone off, and say, "God, I am desperate to hear from You!" It will get you in position to receive the answer. You will witness a miracle take place in your situation.

The Master loves you and would never withhold His answer unless it is for your good. *(Please go back to read and refresh your spirit about the "love" attribute located in the Prayer LAB)*. Get quiet before Him. Your response to the enemy is, "I believe God and stand in resilient faith because my answer is on the way."

- **Be expectant.** This step may be the most challenging. You will feel like giving up because you have waited a long time. Expectation and waiting are somewhat connected. While waiting, be on alert, continue praying relentlessly by standing in agreement, and be disciplined in fasting. Above all, trust God, no matter how the situation looks. He will answer according to His timetable and His divine will for your future.

When an Answer Is Delayed

What do you do when you experience a delay in the waiting room? Consider the following:

First, it may be the Master's way of saying, "The timing is not now." Or "I am working things out for your good; be patient." This is the last thing you wish to hear when you sense that your answer has been delayed. Go back to the Prayer LAB and read the attributes again of God's faithfulness and the covenant He has made with you.

Second, take an inventory of your spiritual closet. This is a great check-up tool. Pray: "Heavenly Father, show me if there is anything that You see in my spiritual life that would delay or prevent the answer to my prayer." The Master appreciates honesty.

This check-up tool reminded me of a story about a scarf I thought was lost, but it was only hidden.

One day, I went to my clothes closet to

look for a red scarf that I needed for a boost of color to a suit. I searched through my scarves that were hung on a special rack to prevent them from falling, but it was not there. Suddenly, the thought occurred to me that it may have fallen to the floor behind the rack. As I knelt and searched, my eye caught a ray of color and I reached back to pull it to me and it was the red scarf. For a moment, the scarf was hidden from view and I began to explore further until I found it.

Will you take time to explore within your heart to see if there is anything that needs to be released? Although this is a story about a hidden scarf, it can be a symbol of a hidden sin. Let's reflect on anything that would cause a delay or could be applied when the Master answered with a "No" or "It's Delayed."

THE SPIRIT OF UNFORGIVENESS

The spirit or attitude of unforgiveness can be one of the offenses that will cause unrest between nations, families to be divided, and church members to scatter. When we harbor or hold unforgiveness against anyone, it grieves the Master's heart and prevents our prayers from being answered and our life's purpose from being fulfilled. (Read Matthew 5:22-25.)

Dr. Martin Luther King, Jr., once said, "Forgiveness is not an occasional act, it is a constant attitude."[2]

Here are two traits of unforgiveness that will hinder your prayer:

1. **Bitterness:** Have you ever tasted something that is bitter or sour? Sometimes, it may leave an aftertaste in your mouth that will last several hours. This is similar to what happens when we do not release those who offend us. Bitterness may linger weeks and even years if we do not

proactively take charge to release those who caused the offense.

2. **<u>Anger</u>:** This is a trait that can become extremely ugly if we lose control and allow our flesh to dominate the situation. The answers we are seeking and expecting God to answer are worth bringing this unruly spirit to the feet of Jesus. His promise found in I John 1:9 (NKJV) is true, "If we confess our sins, He is faithful and just to forgive us our sins to cleanse us from all unrighteousness."

If the wounds of bitterness and anger still remain open, let's pray this short prayer of release and victory, and be set free.

A Prayer of Release and Victory

In the name of Jesus, I speak healing right now over (say the name of whoever has asked for forgiveness). I know that freedom is my portion, and because I chose to forgive (say the name of the person or persons) who offended me. I will watch You work miracles in my life, and You will answer my prayers according to Your will. The blind men who followed Jesus cried out in Matthew 9:27–29 (NKJV), "Son of David, have mercy on us..." Just as Jesus responded to them, "I hear you," Lord, respond to me today by saying, "Be free!" I receive Your freedom in Jesus' name. Amen.

What to Do When God Says No

When a parent says no to their child, it is usually for the child's good. When an employer says no concerning a project you submitted for approval, it may not be time to implement. When a university says no to your college application, it may not be the one you're supposed to attend. God is intentional in His answers. He never makes a mistake. When you hear no, it does not feel good. In your mind, they have become the opponents who are standing in the way of your success and your future. You feel deprived of an opportunity to prove yourself. Or perhaps you feel as if you've done something wrong and the spirit of condemnation appears. These are strategies of your enemy, Satan. Resist him! Shut him down by speaking the promises of God's Word, and refuse to listen to his accusations.

Please be encouraged. God promised never to leave nor forsake you. May I suggest you revisit the Prayer LAB and refresh your mind concerning the attributes of God? Then refocus on God's best for you through His promises as you continue to seek His direction on what to do.

Never Settle

When you are waiting for an answer through prayer, never settle. To settle means you have an "I don't care" attitude. It is like the spirit of defeat. You have allowed the opposing force to have victory over your situation, your life, and future. May I suggest that you go back to the Prayer LAB and read the Master's attributes and study His character? These attributes will remind you of His desire for you to have and be the best. His love for you is unlimited and His faithfulness is enduring.

When you persevere in prayer, you move God's hand to answer your petition. Your answer may come instantly or through a process of time. When you settle, you are saying,

"God cannot do it; why pray again?" Use the time to trust and enter into relentless prayers and remember His promises.

WHAT ARE YOU SPEAKING?

The Book of Proverbs 18:21 (KJV) reads, "Death and life are in the power of the tongue: and they that love it shall eat the fruit thereof."

What are you rehearsing daily to yourself? Are you confessing life over your situation, or death? The Master's Word has power. Once you tap into praying the promises of the Master daily, your life and circumstances will change. It is as God's Word says in Deuteronomy 28:13 (KJV), "And the Lord shall make thee the head, and not the tail; and thou shalt be above only, and thou shalt not be beneath."

My friend, we will confess who the Master says you are and what you can do through Him with this prayer below:

Heavenly Father, You created me in Your image and in Your likeness, therefore, You are mindful of me and my situation. "But thou, O Lord, art a shield for me; my glory, and the lifter up of mine head" (Psalm 3:3, KJV). Your Word says that "I am fearfully and wonderfully made....My substance was not hid from thee, when I was made in secret" (Psalm 139:14-15, KJV). You also said that "I can do all things through Christ which strengtheneth me" (Philippians 4:13, KJV). My talents and gifts will make room for me in Your kingdom. I seal these words with the blood of Jesus. Amen.

Is there a situation from which you need to be released? Are you weary of carrying it? Be as relentless as the widow. Do you pray one time and wait? In Leviticus 6:13 (KJV) we read, "The fire shall ever be burning upon the altar; it shall never go out." May the spirit of prayer be maintained as a continuous fire upon the altar of our hearts. Through persistent worship and thanksgiving, the fire will never cease until you receive the answer!

GOD ANSWERED MY PRAYER FIFTEEN YEARS LATER

After fifteen years had passed since I received my first position in education, God dropped in my heart these words, "It's time to shift; I have not forgotten you." The first position was not my dream job; I just settled. The Britannica Online Dictionary defines *shift* as "to move or to cause (something or someone) to move to a different place, position, etc."[3]

I was uncertain of which way to go, so I began to pray for guidance immediately. My friend, may I encourage you? Never make a major decision until you seek the guidance of the Creator who has the best plan for your life.

The first time I prayed, I received no answer.

Because I knew God's promises, I prayed relentlessly day and night with thanksgiving, while waiting. While praying, He reminded me I had asked Him for a promotion fifteen years ago. The years had passed and I had become content in my current position while helping students. He said to me, "Watch Me work."

I began to feel guilt that I should not move to another position but remain in my present role to see my students (who had been labeled low-functioning) excel. I knew that guilt was a strategy of Satan called condemnation. I rebuked him immediately.

One week later, the Master gave me my answer. No, it was not a trumpet sound but a slight nudge that directed me to a specific school district to view their job postings. Immediately, my eyes landed on a position available that read just like the one I applied for fifteen years earlier in my educational career, but for which I received a rejection letter. As I remembered God's words, "It's time to shift," I moved forward and sent my application to this school district.

Approximately one week later, I received an email to schedule an interview. I knew the Master was working behind the scenes on my behalf. The interview was extremely successful. I was offered the position with a certain salary. I knew immediately that this was not the offer the Master wanted me to accept. Suddenly, I heard in my spirit to ask for a specific salary amount. The amount was more than what they offered the first time. At that moment, the enemy tried to raise doubt in my mind and a slight fear that if I asked for that amount, they would end the job process entirely. I took the risk! Have you ever taken a risk where you may be saying to yourself, *If not now, when*? If the Master said it, I believed Him! I shared with the interviewer the amount that I would accept. The interviewer negotiated back with one thousand dollars more than the last offer.

I became quiet. Then, boldness kicked in and I began to share my experience with the interviewer, including the successes my students achieved, and the ways I could help their students become successful academically. The individual said they would contact me the next day with a final offer. I knew God was working behind the scenes, because I went before Him again in relentless prayer and asked for His anointing with His Word. I confessed His promises back to Him and trusted Him to keep His Word.

The next day, I received the call and they accepted my offer. It was triple the original amount. I could not hold my tears from falling. Praise God, He is truly faithful to keep His promises!

May I take a break here and give you a teachable moment? For those who may not understand when someone has said, "I heard in my spirit" or "Something was laid on my heart," please know that these are just some of the ways that God communicates with His children. First, He can speak to you through an audible voice. Yes, it's as if another person is sitting or standing next to you. Second, He speaks through His Scriptures or promises. Third, He communicates through the spoken word of a friend, minister, or pastor. Last, He can speak to you through your spirit.

As you petition the Master according to His will for you, He will do it. He never lies. Please send us a testimony when the miracle you have been waiting for comes to pass.

THE UNSEEN (HIDDEN) GUEST

While waiting on your answer, an unseen Guest is behind the scenes working on your behalf. He is the righteous Judge, the Master of every situation. He never takes a vacation, slumbers, or falls asleep. He is always on time. His name is Jesus.

It was the widow's persistence in going to the unjust judge that brought her victory.

For a moment, she almost gave up but realized that nothing happens until she moves.
She knew to never settle for the tactics of
the enemy, but to stand in resilient faith. If
you find yourself stuck while waiting, use
one, or all three action steps in this chapter.
Although the situation looks hopeless, do not
give up; a breakthrough is near. Moreover,
like the widow, speak life to your situation.

Imagine if the widow had entered the
Prayer LAB and revisited the character of
the Master. She would have realized that victory was imminent. You too can obtain victory as you sit in the waiting room for your
prayer to be answered. My friend, He has not
forgotten you. He heard you the first time.

A REFLECTIVE MOMENT
OF THE SOUL

Would you take five minutes to reflect over
the past five years of your life? Is there a shift
or transition you knew would have changed

your life for the better if you had taken it? Did you choose to settle? Do you sense an unrest within? I wonder, if you had the opportunity to do it again, would you grasp the moment?

A PRAYER OF PROMISE

John 10:10 (KJV) reads, "The thief cometh not, but for to steal, and to kill, and to destroy: I am come that they might have life, and that they might have it more abundantly." Heavenly Father, help me to seize each moment and opportunity that You have planned for me. With Your guidance, I will not become complacent nor settle for the mediocre when You have created me for greater. Amen.

Chapter Seven

I HEARD YOU

And the Lord said, Hear what
the unjust judge saith.
And shall not God avenge his own
elect, which cry day and night unto
him, though he bear long with them?
—LUKE 18:6-7, KJV

UNTIL NOW, THE Master's voice was silent as He observed the unjust judge's interactions with the widow. Suddenly, in the latter part of verse 6, He speaks, "Hear what the unjust judge saith."

As we read further in the parable, we see that in the latter part of verse 4 and in verse 5, "he said *within* himself, Though I fear not God, nor regard man; Yet because this widow troubleth me, I will avenge her, lest by her continual coming she weary me."

Is it fair to say that the unjust judge's decision to give up the tug of war with the widow and grant her justice was one of defeat?

As the judge walked back to his chamber, one can only imagine how he must have felt after he released her from her adversary. Did the words come back to haunt him as he reflected, "You must be crazy to give in to her request. What were you thinking? She means nothing to you."

Suddenly, he visualized the times that she visited his chambers and his court to ask for help. "I've had enough of her continuous and constant visits. She just keeps bothering me. The only way to get rid of her is to grant her request," he said vehemently to himself.

Remember, this is an officer of the court who has allowed himself to become overpowered and overwhelmed by a mere widow whom he cared nothing about, but suddenly he gave in to her appeal.

Clearly, the widow learned that the key to receiving the answer to her prayer was persistence. Unlike the unjust judge, who had to receive continuous visits from the widow to get justice, the righteous Judge hears His children, the chosen ones, when we cry out to Him day and night and He is present to answer our prayer. In a true sense, this is how the Master feels about us, His chosen; when we call His name, He hears us. Can we dig deeper to find out why the Master is passionate about answering your prayer?

A Covenant Right

In verse 7 of chapter 18, Luke clearly states that not only will the Master, the righteous Judge, avenge or bring justice to His own if they cry out to Him, but He will also bear long with them. It is a covenant right. According to

Britannica Dictionary, the word *bear* means to "to accept or endure (something)."[1]

The use of the word *bear* can be seen in the relationship or interaction between parents and their children.

Parents are special people—special in the sense that many give support to their children with little thought of their own well-being or the sacrifice to ensure that their children thrive through the stages of development and the challenges that they face in life.

Some give their child several chances to learn from their mistakes before consequences are enforced. The goal is not only for them to learn but also to grow from their experiences. And, ultimately, they need to know that you care and will be there for them when they cry out for help. This is how the Master feels about us, His children. When you call His name, He hears you. Just as the parent helps their child through struggles, the righteous Judge has a special attribute called long-suffering, which means He is very patient with us.

Let's recap as we draw a brief mental image of the widow's dilemma. The widow's desire was to be delivered from an oppressor who had caused her much emotional distress. She had no one to help her with the situation, little money, and apparently few friends.

Perhaps prior to the death of her husband, she was seen by her friends as a gentle and private woman with a passive nature. This out-of-control behavior they were witnessing was out of character for her. She had not confided in them about her situation except to inquire if they knew anyone in the justice system who could help her resolve a terrible problem.

One day, she was so distraught that she went to the courthouse in her city to ask for help. Her continual cry for help led her to receive assistance from an unnamed judge.

Little did she know, this judge did not care about man, nor reverence God. He ignored her as if her problem was insignificant.

She continued to pursue him every day, to request that he give her justice from her adversary. Although he did not care for her or her dilemma, verse 5 says that he granted her justice because he became weary of the widow's continuous pursuit. Her victory was gained through the power of her voice: relentless praying and resilient faith.

In this verse, Luke presents to the reader a powerful, thought-provoking illustration that contrasts how the righteous Judge responds when we cry out to Him in prayer, "And shall not God avenge his own elect, which cry day and night unto him, though he bear long with them?" (Luke 18:7, KJV).

It is evident in this parable that the unjust judge was callous, unconcerned, and downright rude to the widow and her needs. Yet the righteous Judge, our Master, who is just and faithful never becomes weary when His children, the chosen, cry out to Him when in need.

Many individuals who live in various countries around the world are experiencing persecution as the widow portrayed in this parable. Missionaries in foreign countries have lost their lives because they obeyed the Great Commission. Corrie Ten Boom once said, "Jesus did not promise to change the circumstances around us. He promised great peace and pure joy to those who would learn to believe that God actually controls all things."[2]

Furthermore, Luke 18:7 shows the heart of our heavenly Father toward His children when we cry out to Him sincerely in prayer. God loves you so much, and He has promised to defend and deliver you. As His children, it is our covenant right to receive all the promises that He has for us.

As His chosen, we have a covenant right to

receive the answer to our prayer. We have a covenant right to His promise found in Psalm 84:11 (KJV), "No good *thing* will he withhold from them that walk uprightly." When you choose to make the Master the Lord of your life, to serve Him and put no other gods before Him, you have entered into a covenant or an agreement. He is faithful, and He keeps His covenant.

Shall we explore a few biblical stories of how the Master demonstrated His immeasurable love towards those who pursued Him with the power of relentless prayer and stood in resilient faith until they received the answer? You will witness how the Master protected and endured long with them, then finally sent deliverance. As you activate your faith, remember the words of the Master in Luke 1:37 (KJV): "For with God nothing shall be impossible."

He Did It Before—Watch Him Do It Again

The first example is found in Acts 10:1-4 (NKJV), where a centurion named Cornelius was noted as a devout man who prayed daily. The Bible says he prayed and gave charitable contributions to the poor. The poor are one of the groups listed under the Master's providential care. (Refer to chapter 3 of this book.)

One day, the centurion had a vision, and the angel of God came to him and said in verse 4, "Your prayers and your alms have come up for a memorial before God." His prayers were pleasing to God! They were satisfying. God heard his prayer immediately.

If Cornelius prayed, and God heard him, then will He not hear your prayer when you cry out to Him? If He did it for you before, He will certainly do it again. We cannot give up or give in. Expect to receive your answer. We will show another example of the love that God has for His people through deliverance during the midnight hour.

Midnight

Midnight is the darkest part of night when our senses are heightened and our emotions are fragile. Spiritually, when we experience midnight, that's when Satan attacks our mind to believe that the Master will not bring us through or answer our prayer.

My friend, this is an important time to pray relentlessly. What is significant about midnight in your life? Could it symbolize a time of testing or transition in your life, or a point of deliverance to receive your answered prayer?

Do not give up, give in, or settle. Persist with resilient faith. Midnight can be anytime in your life when you see no way out! Are you experiencing midnight in your life? When we call out to God earnestly day and night, He is always there to hear us.

Another midnight example that shows the significant power of relentless prayer and resilient faith is found in Acts 16:25. Paul and Silas had a midnight hour experience while praying and singing praises to God. Suddenly, a great earthquake shook the foundation of the prison and all the doors swung open and everyone's chains fell off.

It was a lot like when the Children of Israel had experienced deliverance in Exodus 12:29 (NIV), "At midnight the Lord struck down all the firstborn in Egypt." The children of Israel cried out to God because of their continued oppression at the hand of Pharaoh, the hard taskmaster. God heard His children cry out to Him and He delivered them. The Master did not forget His children, neither has He forgotten you.

Have you ever had a midnight experience where a friend knocks on your door to ask for help?

Luke 11:5-8 illustrates a powerful prayer

of persistence. An individual knocks on his friend's door to request three loaves of bread for a guest who had arrived from a journey. The friend does not open the door but speaks to him from inside saying, "Don't bother me. The door is already locked, and my children and I are in bed" (NIV). His friend kept knocking out of an urgent need until his friend got up and gave him what he requested.

God can deliver you too from the hand of the adversary if you are relentless in prayer. Remember, according to *Merriam-Webster's Dictionary*, *relentless* is defined as "not easing up or slackening, maintaining speed or unyielding."[3] It is a mountain-moving, gushing-from-the-belly prayer that will move heaven and shake hell to receive your answer.

Remember, a waiting room is just a temporary holding area. It is only for a season; you are not meant to wait there forever.

In my spirit, I feel a change is coming in

your life. Do you feel it? Your answer is here. Reach up and receive it. How do you receive it? Find a promise in His Word and confess it over and over, then go to chapter 6 in this book and grasp the action steps of agreement, fasting, and expectancy. Pray this prayer:

> *Thank You, heavenly Father, for answering my prayer. You are faithful to meet our needs. Apostle Paul admonishes us in Hebrews 4:16 (KJV) to "come boldly unto the throne of grace, that we may obtain mercy, and find grace to help in time of need." So, thank You for the experience in the waiting room. It has taught me how to travail relentlessly and stand in resilient faith. In Jesus' name, amen.*

While in prayer, learn to go to God for your brothers and sisters who need deliverance out of the hands of their persecutors and oppressors. Pray for our community, our state, nation, and then the world. Keep praying. Give God no rest. He has given us an open heaven. He heard your cry the first time, but you should continue to seek Him.

If He heard Daniel who prayed *three times a day* to be delivered because he would not honor the decree given by the king to bow down to man, and he continued to worship and serve the only true and living God, Jehovah (see Daniel 6:10), then my friend, the Master has heard you too, because you are also His chosen, His elect.

A REFLECTIVE MOMENT OF THE SOUL

Can you think of a time when you prayed and your prayer was delayed? In that moment, how did you feel? As you have matured in your journey of prayer, is there anything you would have done differently to receive an answer?

A Prayer of Promise

Heavenly Father, 1 John 5:14-15 (author's paraphrase) states, "And this is the confidence that I have, if I ask anything according to Your Will, You hear me; and if I know that You hear me, I have the petition that I have requested of You." Thank You that my petition has been answered. Amen.

Chapter Eight
A STATE OF URGENCY

*I tell you that he will avenge them
speedily. Nevertheless when the Son of man
cometh, shall he find faith on the earth?*
—LUKE 18:8, KJV

ᴇᴀᴄʜ sᴛᴀᴛᴇ ɪs responsible for having an emergency plan in place for when a catastrophic event happens. The purpose is to alert the citizens to be on guard for major conflicts such as a state or world health crisis, civil protests that erupt out of control, or natural disasters such as earthquakes and tornadoes that could lead to loss of life and property.

The alert can happen through a gradual

process or suddenly. "Once the command is given from the law enforcement, city officers or world leaders, protections for its citizens" goes into effect speedily to guard them from impending danger.[1]

Luke concludes this parable with a second application in the latter part of verse 8 with an urgency and reassurance to the believer.

God who is a righteous Judge, will defend His chosen, His elect, quickly from the enemy when they call upon Him. This is so unlike the actions of the unjust judge who would not help the widow until she wore him out through persistence. Luke continues with an emphasis on the word *speedily* in verse 8 to establish within the heart of the believer the position of waiting with expectancy—never giving up nor doubting that the Master will answer your prayer or send help in time of need. In Numbers 23:19 (KJV), Moses reminds us that, "God *is* not a man, that he should lie; neither the son of man, that he should repent: hath he said, and shall he not do it? or hath he spoken, and shall he not make it good?"

TROUBLED ON EVERY SIDE

Apostle Paul penned in 2 Corinthians 4:8-9 (KJV), "We are troubled on every side, yet not distressed; we *are* perplexed, but not in despair; persecuted, but not forsaken; cast down, but not destroyed..." In Luke 18:8 (KJV), Luke asks the most significant and profound question in this parable: "...when the Son of man cometh, shall he find faith on the earth?" Why does he ask if God can "find faith on earth?" In contrast, in Luke 18:1 (KJV), Luke pens, "That men ought always to pray, and not to faint."

In the introduction, I shared with the reader that faith was the force that activates you to receive the answer to your prayer. My friend, it is crucial that you stand strong in your faith as you wait for His return. John reminds us that "The thief cometh not, but for to steal, and to kill, and to destroy..." (John 10:10, KJV). Remember, the thief is your opposing force who does not desire you to have abundant life, but to live in chaos and confusion and to doubt that God cares about you.

Verses 1 and 8 are somewhat connected in thought as Luke admonishes us to pray always, not faint, and then asks when the Son of man comes, will He find faith on earth? God created mankind. He knows the heart and nature of His creatures.

He knows man is weak, "but the people that do know their God shall be strong, and do *exploits*" (Daniel 11:32, KJV, emphasis added). He knows we have an enemy who would strive to steal, kill, and destroy our destiny if we are not praying constantly and standing with resilient faith watching for His Second Coming.

A PANORAMIC VIEW OF HIS COMING (TIMELINE)

You may be asking, "When was His first appearance?" He came when mankind, His creation, needed a savior, a deliverer, and a redeemer.[2] He was born in a state of lowliness, wrapped in swaddling clothes by His parents, and laid in a manger, according to the Scriptures. (See Luke 2:11-12.)

As Jesus grew from youth to manhood, He had roughly three years to fulfill His purpose in the earth. After that, He was crucified, buried in a tomb, and rose again.

He reminded His disciples that He would ascend to heaven to prepare a place for His chosen, the elect, who were committed to serving Him with all their heart, soul, mind, and strength. (See Mark 12:30.)

Moreover, upon His departure, He left instructions in Luke 18:1 (The Message, emphasis added), "...it was necessary for them to *pray consistently and never quit.*" My friend, the Master is soon to return. Mark 13:32 (NIV) reads, "But about that day or hour no one knows, not even the angels in heaven, nor the Son, but only the Father."

Jesus will not return in a state of ambiguity as He was born. This event will be according to the scripture in Revelation 1:7 (NKJV), "Behold, He is coming with clouds, and every eye will see Him..."

In Matthew 24:27 (KJV), His coming will be glorious, "For as the lightning cometh out of the east, and shineth even unto the west; so shall also the coming of the Son of man be."

The question is, Shall He find His chosen, the believer, still holding on through faith? Will you still be found witnessing, praying, encouraging your brothers and sisters, visiting the sick, and more?

Matter of Emergency

What's more, Hebrews 11:6 (KJV) encourages the readers by saying, "But without faith *it is* impossible to please *him*: for he that cometh to God must believe that he is, and that he is a rewarder of them that diligently seek him." When He returns, will He find you working in His kingdom? My friend, He needs your hands, your feet, and your voice to reach the lost, and He wants you to remain resilient in your faith.

Is there an urgency for you to fulfill the assignment that He has created you do? Will He find you still sharing the good news of His saving grace with others and working to prepare them for the kingdom? Can He trust you to intercede for those who are being persecuted for their faith, and who are facing tragedies and devastations in our world? His desire is to say, "Well done" when He finds you praying relentlessly for His bride, the church.

Our world is in trouble. As Timothy admonishes in 2 Timothy 3:2-4 (KJV), "For men shall be lovers of their own selves, covetous, boasters, proud, blasphemers, disobedient to parents, unthankful, unholy, Without natural affection, trucebreakers, false accusers, incontinent, fierce, despisers of those that are good, traitors, heady, highminded, lovers of pleasures more than lovers of God."

As His disciples on Earth, how can we prepare for His imminent return? Ultimately, God wants to know that He can count on His chosen, His elect, to be relentless in prayer, and standing resilient in faith to receive the answer to their prayers.

Reflective Moment of the Soul

Can you remember a moment where you experienced an emergency that you needed a prayer to be answered immediately and it was delayed? With that in mind, think of a time you prayed and the Master answered quickly. Contrast the two and share with a friend if anything was done differently to receive your answer.

A Prayer of Promise

Heavenly Father, Revelation 3:20 (AMP) is a commandment of promise, "Behold I stand at the door [of the church] and continually knock. If anyone hears My voice and opens the door, I will come in and eat with him (restore him), and he with Me."

Conclusion
YOUR MISSION

THE INSTRUCTIONS THAT the Master gave His disciples prior to His departure to prepare a place for them was "...at all times they ought to pray and not give up and lose heart" (Luke 18:1, AMP).

These words were spoken over two thousand years ago but are still very relevant to us today. As believers, and His disciples, we are waiting for His return also, and we should always pray without ceasing to receive the answer to our prayers.

Just as the widow in this parable experienced the abuse and injustice at the hands of her adversary, we too will suffer persecution and many things while waiting for the

Master's return. Nevertheless, the key to the widow's victory was persistence in prayer. She was relentless in her request for help.

Nothing will happen to change your situation unless you pray consistently. In Proverbs 18:21 (AMP), King Solomon expressed so vividly how your confession will change the course of your prayer life: "Death and life are in the power of the tongue." When you choose to speak life through the power of prayer, you will witness chains of addictions broken, those who are bound will be set free, bodies and minds will be healed of incurable diseases, and communities will be transformed. When you speak or pray negative words over your situation, the condition will worsen and your dreams will die. For that reason, I encourage you to pray with power and stand strong in resilient faith.

Remember, God hears you and desires to answer when you cry out to Him. There are times that the answer may be delayed, but never give up. Be aware of the evil one who will come to abort the answer to prevent it from manifesting in your life.

Do not carry unforgiveness. It's toxic. It will prevent you from receiving the answer you have been waiting for, not only for you but also for others. Do not become over-whelmed by the cares of this life or be caught off guard by His imminent return. I implore you to stay on fire for God through prayer. Matthew 24:12 (KJV) reads, "And because iniquity shall abound, the love of many shall wax cold." A state of emergency is being sounded across the world. Matthew 24:7 (KJV) admonishes, "For nation shall rise against nation, and kingdom against kingdom: and there shall be famines, and pestilences, and earthquakes, in divers places."

Stay in the Prayer LAB. *Learn* about the Master's attributes and character so you can pray with the knowledge and wisdom of who He is while you wait for the answer.

In the same way, learn how to *ASK* as the acronym we discussed in chapter 4 suggests. Be specific with your request, not double-minded. Then *believe* your answer is coming. Hebrews 11:6 (KJV) says, "But without faith it is impossible to please *him*: for he that cometh to God must believe that he is, and that he is a rewarder of them that diligently seek him."

When we pray, we can expect an answer, which is the reward of our prayers. In this last hour, will you mobilize and prepare to stand on the front line for others who are unable to pray for themselves? Can He count on you to pray always and not give up?

Appendix A
MEDITATE DAILY ON GOD'S PROMISES

(All scriptures are quoted from the King James Version)

And the LORD, he it is that doth go before thee; he will be with thee, he will not fail thee, neither forsake thee: fear not, neither be dismayed.

—DEUTERONOMY 31:8

For this child I prayed; and the LORD hath given me my petition which I asked of him.

—1 SAMUEL 1:27

So we fasted and besought our God for this: and he was intreated of us.

—EZRA 8:23

In the time of their trouble, when they cried unto thee, thou heardest them from heaven.

—Nehemiah 9:27

The LORD is far from the wicked: but he heareth the prayer of the righteous.

—Proverbs 15:29

Thou wilt keep him in perfect peace, whose mind is stayed *on* thee: because he trusteth in thee.

—Isaiah 26:3

Seek ye the LORD while he may be found, call upon him while he is near.

—Isaiah 55:6

And ye shall seek me, and find me, when ye shall search for me with all your heart.

—Jeremiah 29:13

Again I say unto you, That if two of you shall agree on earth as touching any thing that they shall ask, it shall be done for them of my Father which is in heaven.

—MATTHEW 18:19

The word is nigh thee, even in thy mouth, and in thy heart: that is, the word of faith which we preach.

—ROMANS 10:8

For there is no difference between the Jew and the Greek: for the same Lord over all is rich unto all that call upon him.

—ROMANS 10:12

Without faith it is impossible to please him.

—HEBREWS 11:6

The prayer of the faith shall save the sick, and the Lord shall raise them up.

—James 5:15

For the eyes of the Lord are over the righteous, and his ears are open unto their prayers: but the face of the Lord is against them that do evil.

—1 Peter 3:12

And whatsoever we ask, we receive of him, because we keep his commandments, and do those things that are pleasing in his sight.

—1 John 3:22

Appendix B
A PRACTICE PRAYER LAB ACTIVITY

(See chapter 5.)

Section 1

1. Write one prayer request:

_____

_____

2. The letter L in LAB means to:

_____

3. The letter A in LAB means to:

_____

4. The letter B in LAB means to:

_____

5. List one attribute or characteristic you learned about the Master:

_____

6. When asking God for something, be: (see page 73)

_____

7. The word *belief* is a cousin to: (see page 76)

_____

Section 2

8. Write one or more promises in God's Word that affirms your prayer request. For

example: you are unemployed and need food (Ps. 23:1; Phil. 4:19).

(Answer Key: 2. L-Learn, 3. A-Abide, 4. B-Believe; 6. specific, 7. faith)

NOTES

INTRODUCTION

1. Merriam-Webster.com, s.v., "power," https://www.merriam-webster.com/dictionary/power).

2. Merriam-Webster.com, s.v., "resilient," https://www.merriam-webster.com/dictionary/resilient.

3. Dictionary.com, s.v. "relentless," https://www.dictionary.com/browse/relentless.

CHAPTER 1: SETTING THE SCENE

1. W. E. Vine, MA, *Vines Expository Dictionary of NT Words* (McLean Virginia: MacDonald Publishing Company), 65, s.v. *Apostolos, Apostle,* "one sent forth."

2. Ibid., 210-211, s.v. *Parousia*, "Coming, Arrival or Presence."

3. Goodreads.com, "Norman Vincent Peale Quotes," https://www.goodreads.com/author/quotes/8435.Norman_Vincent_Peale?page=4.

4. Finis Jennings Dake, *Dake's Annotated Reference Bible* (Lawrenceville, GA: Dake Bible Sales, 1961), 18.

5. *I Dream of Jeannie,* a popular television comedy aired in the mid-1960s. The main character used her gift to make things appear and disappear with her make believe powers.

6. W. E. Vine, MA, *Vines Expository Dictionary of NT Words* (McLean Virginia: MacDonald Publishing Company), 840, s.v. *Parabole, Parable.*

7. Ibid.

8. Dictionary.com, s.v., "command," https://www.dictionary.com/browse/command.

Chapter 3: The Widow's Plight

1. Merriam Webster, s.v. "adversary," https://www.merriam-webster.com/dictionary/adversary.

2. Mark Johnson, "Five Things about Covid We Still Don't Understand at Our Peril," *The Washington Post*, September 26, 2022 as quoted by Yahoo News, https://news.yahoo.com/

five-things-covid-still-dont-130023988.
html?fr=sycsrp_catchall.

3. Spurgeon.org, "6 Things Spurgeon Didn't
Say," August 24, 2016, www.spurgeon.
org/resource-library/blog-entries/6-things-
spurgeon-didnt-say/.

CHAPTER 4: BEING RELENTLESS PAYS OFF

1. Stanford Graduate School of Business,
"Making First & Lasting Impressions,"
February 7, 2018, www.youtube.com/
watch?v=ukWxfL7cBw0.

2. Dictionary.com, s.v., "knock," https://www.
dictionary.com/browse/knock.

CHAPTER 5: THE PRAYER LAB

1. Alane Lim, Ben Biggs, "What is
Chemistry?," LiveScience.com, November
5, 2021, https://www.livescience.
com/45986-what-is-chemistry.html.

2. Sarah Christmyer, "Create in Me
a Clean Heart: Ten Minutes a
Day in the Penitential Psalms,"
www.goodreads.com/work/

quotes/49140744-create-in-me-a-clean-heart-ten-minutes-a-day-in-the-penitential-psalms.

3. Merriam Webster.com, s.v. "abide," https://www.merriam-webster.com/dictionary/abide.

4. Dictionary.com, s.v. "faith," https://www.dictionary.com/browse/faith.

5. Dictionary.com, s.v. "believe," https://www.dictionary.com/browse/believe.

6. Dictionary.com, s.v. "proof," https://www.dictionary.com/browse/proof.

Chapter 6: Nothing Will Happen Until You Move

1. Goodreads.com, "Albert Einstein," https://www.goodreads.com/author/show/9810.Albert_Einstein.

2. Goodreads.com, "Martin Luther King Jr. Quotes," https://www.goodreads.com/author/quotes/23924.Martin_Luther_King_Jr_.

3. The Britannica Dictionary, s.v. "shift," https://www.britannica.com/dictionary/shift-.

Chapter 7: I Heard You

1. The Britannica Dictionary, s.v. "bear," https://www.britannica.com/dictionary/bear.

2. AZ Quotes, "Corrie Ten Boom Quotes About Jesus," https://www.azquotes.com/author/1659-Corrie_Ten_Boom/tag/jesus.

3. Dictionary.com, s.v. "relentless," https://www.dictionary.com/browse/relentless.

Chapter 8: A Matter of Urgency

1. Kirsten Barber, "What Does a State of Emergency Actually Mean?" North Carolina Department of Public Safety, December 14, 2018, https://www.ncdps.gov/blog/2018/12/14/what-does-state-emergency-actually-mean.

2. Curt Landry Ministries, "Jesus: Redeemer, Deliverer, and Savior of the World," December 13, 2020, https://www.curtlandry.com/jesus-redeemer-deliverer-and-savior-of-the-world/.

ABOUT THE AUTHOR

Doris E. Golder is the president of D'Vine Strategies LLC. She is the visionary strategist who trains, equips, and motivates individuals to discover, be released, and walk in their purpose. She is an advocate for those who feel voiceless. She has conducted workshops on prayer, youth development, and gifts of grace. Doris has a heart for the heavy mandate that pastors carry in these End Times.

Doris was the founder and servant leader for Travailing Ministries International Inc. (TMII), a nonprofit organization from 2009-2018. The organization held workshops on spiritual development, assisted youth with book scholarships, and provided community and humanitarian resources.

Doris utilizes prayer as her platform, recognizing that faith and prayer are the power sources that please and move the hand of God.

An ordained minister and chaplain, Doris has earned a bachelor of arts degree in business management, and a master's degree in urban ministry with a concentration in marriage and family. She is a K-12 school counselor.

CONTACT INFORMATION
Website: www.dvinestrategies.com
Email: doris@dvinestrategies.com

ANOTHER BOOK BY DORIS GOLDER
Gifts of Grace: Seven Keys to Discovering Your Hidden Potential

Printed in the USA
CPSIA information can be obtained
at www.ICGtesting.com
LVHW071147260424
778527LV00016B/270